A Special Gift

_____

Presented To

_____

From

_____

Date

from my favorite daughter
February, 2006

Dedicated to my family - Rod,
Rodney and Carla, Jamie and Bracken,
Audrey, Adalyn and Aiden.

Thanks to all my family and friends who encouraged me and cheered me on to the finish. Thanks to my new and fondest brother in the Lord, Scott, who has endured my changes and my challenges writing this book.

©2005 by Jane Gray

Scripture quotations are taken from the Holy Bible, New International Version.

Design and Editorial Services by: Scott & Juli Cook

Cover Photo: Photodisc

Photography by: Jane Gray

ISBN: 0-977-00865-7

Printed in Mexico

Please visit our website www.dontwait.com.

Don't Wait

take the first step

JANE GRAY

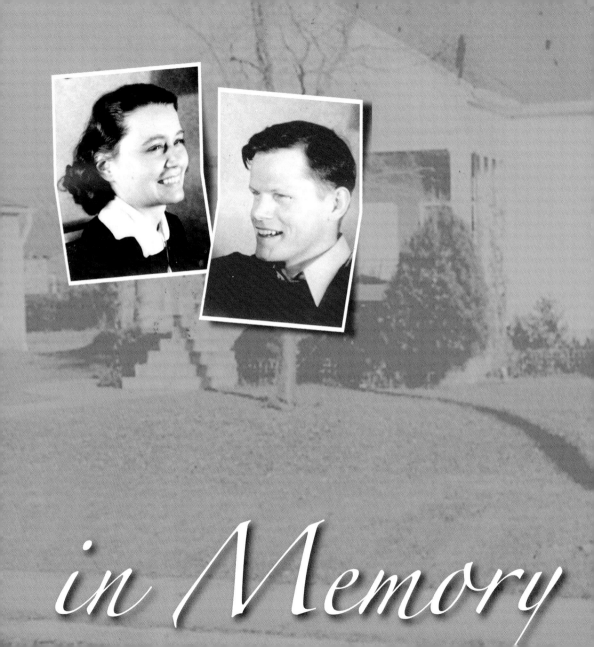

in Memory

All my love to my Mom and Dad .

All the honor and glory to our
Lord Jesus Christ

Can you ever remember a time when you regretted having said a kind word?

ANONYMOUS

Don't

*H*ow many times have you found yourself wondering why didn't I...?

If only I would have... If I had just known...

If I could do it all over again... and the list goes on and on.

Wait...

But whoever lives by the truth comes into the light, so that it may be seen plainly that what he has done has been done through God.

John 3:21

Why do we let things go undone or wait to make something right that is wrong? Why don't we take that extra step and finish the task we know we need to do?

I can do all things through Christ which strengthens me.

Philippians 4:13

take the first

After seventeen years of
saying the words Don't Wait
and never taking the first step,
I've decided it is time to share
what I've learned to hopefully
give you the incentive not to
wait as well.

As we walk the
paths of our
unknown with your
gracious love you
will show us the way.

Anonymous

step...

All your sons
will be taught by
the LORD , and
great will be your
children's peace.

Isaiah 54:13

People know me as a caretaker, a friend, definitely a mother and now a grandmother. My spiritual foundation came from my parents and my mother's sister. Their unconditional love supported me all throughout my life.

Train up a child in the way he should go and when he is old he will not depart from it.

Proverbs 22:6

It is from feeling deep emotion
and life that I am finally sharing
these two life-changing words
that I received from the Lord at
the death of my dad in 1989—

"Don't Wait!"

If I had a rose for every time I thought
of you I'd walk through a garden.

Author Unknown

Honor thy father and thy mother that thy days may be long upon the land which the Lord thy God giveth thee.

Exodus 20:17

Children's children are a crown to the aged, and parents are the pride of their children .

Proverbs 17:6

If your words have cheered one failing heart, kindled anew one fading after fire, your work is not a failure; chords are touched that will re-echo from the angel choir.

Author Unknown

When I was given this message, I thought it meant I shouldn't wait to tell my dad I loved him before he died.

Seek first

After that, it seemed to me above all else, Don't Wait to tell someone you love them should be everyone's top priority.

Trust in the Lord with all thine heart; and lean not unto thine own understanding. In all thy ways acknowledge Him, and He shall direct thy paths..
Proverbs 3:5-6

As life has gone on I've come to understand that these words apply to countless other situations. I've learned that they are not only important in the physical aspects of our life but also in the spirit of our souls.

Dear friend, I pray that you may enjoy good health and that all may go well with you, even as your soul is getting along well.

3 John 1:2

. . . . *the*

There are many things
in life that catch your
eye but only a few will
catch your heart.

Author Unknown

Kingdom

A rose speaks of love silently in a language known only to the heart.

Author Unknown

People don't want to talk about their souls anymore.

They would rather talk about material things than about their spiritual inner being.

Do material things really matter when facing illness, death or other major life trials?

nothing

Take my yoke upon you
and learn from me, for I am
gentle and humble in heart,
and you will find rest for
your souls.

Matthew 11:29

else matters.

When my mother died, I realized in a larger sense, the importance of not waiting to spend time or effort on relationships. No amount of material wealth or possessions could replace the depth of spiritual love, communication and understanding I had known with my mother.

Mother means selfless devotion, limitless sacrifice, and love that passes understanding.

Author Unknown

The fruit of the spirit is love, joy, peace, patience, kindness, generosity, faithfulness, gentleness, and self control.

Galatians 5:22

A mother's heart holds many charms and love is ever in her arms and her eyes a faith divine. A home is yours, mother mine.

Anonymous

And hope does not disappoint us, because God has poured out His love into our hearts by the Holy Spirit, whom He has given us.

Romans 5:5

God's

Fortunately, in the last week of her life I have the memory of singing Jesus Loves Me together with her while driving in the car.

Where there is great love, there are always miracles.

Author Unknown

presence . . .

No eye has seen, no ear has heard,
no mind has conceived what God has
prepared for those who love Him.

1 Corinthians 2:9

is everywhere.

On the night she died, I took the last steps with my mother here on earth. Tragically during our last walk together she had a massive heart attack and fell before my eyes. As I kneeled next to her, she laid without breathing. My mother was home with the Lord.

Thank you, Jesus, for placing me there at the end of this special mother's life.

Not until each loom
is silent

And the shutters
cease to fly

Will God unroll
the pattern

And explain the
reason why

The dark threads are
as needful

In the weavers
skillful hand

As the threads of
gold and silver

For the pattern which
He planned.

Anonymous

But store up for yourselves treasures in heaven, where moth and rust do not destroy, and where thieves do not break in and steal. For where your treasure is, there your heart will be also.

Matthew 6:20-21

Grief and sorrow laid heavy on my heart. Amazingly the first night after losing her, I experienced the warmth of God's presence in a way I had never known before. This gave me a deeper longing for eternity and a closer relationship with God.

Love
What is love?
No one can define it.
It's something so great
Only God could design it.

Yes, love is beyond
what man can define
for love is immortal
and God's gift is devine.

Author Unknown

The sadness of my mother's death took me down another road. God has carried me on this journey, and His sweet blessings of sorrow taught me to keep my eyes on Jesus.

I finally understood the need to pursue both the spiritual and eternal aspects of life in the busyness of everyday living. Through both trials and blessing my message is simple — Don't Wait!

Follow the way of love and eagerly desire spiritual gifts, especially the gift of prophecy.

1 Corinthians 14 :1

I will lift my eyes to the hills—where does my help come from? My help comes from the Lord the Master of heaven and earth.

Psalm 121:1-2

Life is a journey, not a home, a road, not a city of habitation, and the enjoyments and blessings we have are but little inns on the roadside of life, where we may be refreshed for a moment, that with new strength we may push on...to the rest that remaineth for the people of God.

Anonymous

I am the way and
the truth and
the life. No one
comes to the
Father except
through me.

John 14:6

Don't Wait
to put God
first in your
life!

"Yes, it is as you say," Jesus replied. "But I say to all of you: In the future you will see the Son of Man sitting at the right hand of the Mighty One and coming on the clouds of heaven."

Matthew 26:64

Wonderful name He bares

Wonderful crown He wears

Wonderful blessing His triumphs afford

Wonderful calvary

Wonderful grace for the wonderful love of my wonderful Lord.

Author Unknown

Live a God centered life.

Develop a Christ-like character.

Bring honor to God.

Praise Him from sunrise to sunset.

Don't Wait to live for God's purpose.

He is the image of the invisible God, the firstborn over all creation. For by Him all things were created: things in heaven and on earth, visible and invisible, whether thrones or powers or rulers or authorities, all things were created by Him and for Him. He is before all things, and in Him all things hold together.

Colossians 1:15-17

Nails could not have kept Jesus on the cross had love not kept him there.

Author Unknown

Have a personal relationship with Jesus.

Live by God's word.

God created you for His purpose, not your own.

God planned eternity for everyone.

Let us fix our eyes on Jesus, the author and perfecter of our faith, who for the joy set before Him endured the cross, scorning its shame, and sat down at the right hand of the throne of God.

Hebrews 12:2

Having someone who understands you is home. Having someone who loves you is belonging. Having both is a blessing.

Anonymous

Thank God for life.

Therefore everyone who hears these words of mine and puts them into practice is like a wise man who built his house on the rock. The rain came down, the streams rose, and the winds blew and beat against the house; yet it did not fall because it had its foundation on the rock.

Matthew 7:24-25

Don't Wait to be thankful.

Thank your family for their love and support.

Thank your minister, preacher or your priest.

A new command I give you: Love one another. As I have loved you, so you must love one another .

John 13:34

Friends are angels who lift our feet when our own wings have trouble remembering how to fly.

Author Unknown

Thank your friends for being there when you've needed them.

Thank missionaries for spreading God's word.

A friend loveth at all times.

Proverbs 17:17

The promise
is for you and
your children
and for all who
are far off—for
all whom the
Lord our God
will call.

Acts 2:39

You cannot always have happiness
but you can always give happiness.

Anonymous

Don't Wait to bless others.

Give your spouse a word of praise.

Read scripture to your children.

Be a messenger of God's word.

Take a meal to someone you've been thinking about.

Teach prayers to your kids
and grandkids.

The gift is small
But love is all.

Author Unknown

Say I love you.

Give to the less fortunate.

Involve yourself in a community project.

Do not repay evil with evil or insult with insult, but with blessing , because to this you were called so that you may inherit a blessing.

1 Peter 3:9

Whoever serves me must follow me; and where I am, my servant also will be. My Father will honor the one who serves me.

John 12:26

Be devoted to one another in brotherly love. Honor one another above yourselves.

Romans 12:10

I wrote your name in the sand but the waves washed it away. Then I wrote it in the sky but the wind blew it away. So I wrote it in my heart and that's where it will stay.

Author Unknown

Don't Wait to honor someone in the military.

Send a letter to a service member.

Do something special for their family members at home.

Pray for all serving our country.

Pray for our leaders.

We loved you so much that we were delighted to share with you not only the gospel of God but our lives as well, because you had become so dear to us.

1 Thessalonians 2:8

Faith, hope and love—the greatest of these is Love.

Make it a top priority.

Chances of opportunity and circumstances change.

The best expression of love is your time.

A letter can be read and reread. It calms and soothes the sometimes turbulent waters of friendship. A letter once a part of the writer now becomes a part of the recipient. Outside of our actual presence it is the best physical proof we can offer of our friendship, our care and concern for another.

Anonymous

Let love and
faithfulness
never leave
you; bind them
around your
neck, write
them on the
tablet of your
heart.

Proverbs 3:3

Love is blind.
Friendship closes its eyes.

Anonymous

Don't Wait to surround yourself with people you love and who love you.

Join a Bible based church.

Love all your brothers and sisters in Christ.

Share God's love with others.

Love all of your family and friends.

Don't Wait to do tomorrow what you can do today.

Repent, pray, read His holy word daily.

Do not let this Book of the Law depart from your mouth; meditate on it day and night, so that you may be careful to do everything written in it. Then you will be prosperous and successful.

Joshua 1:8

Accept Jesus as your Lord and Savior.

Walk in Gods word.

Witness to others.

Faith is not knowing what the future holds but knowing who holds the future.

Author unknown

But grow in the grace and knowledge of our Lord and Savior Jesus Christ. To Him be glory both now and forever! Amen.

2 Peter 3:18

Pray without ceasing

1 Thessalonians 5:17

The real secret of happiness is not what you give or what you receive; it's what you share.

Anonymous

Don't Wait to live in God's Glory.

Recognize that everything was created by God.

Honor and praise God for all He has given us.

Live to reflect the light of God.

Worship Him daily.

Don't Wait to Please God.

Blessed is the man who finds wisdom,
the man who gains understanding, for
he is more profitable than silver and
yields better returns than gold.

Proverbs 3:13

Commit yourself completely to Jesus.

Be what God created you to be.

Store treasures in heaven.

Be kind and humble.

Appreciate all of God's beauty.

Some people come into our lives and quickly go. Some stay for awhile and leave footprints on our heart and we are never ever the same.

Author Unknown

Here I am! I stand at the door and knock. If anyone hears my voice and opens the door, I will come in and eat with him, and he with me.

Revelations 3:20

One who sleeps under a quilt is comforted with love.

Author Unknown

Don't Wait to give of yourself.

Be a steward of God.

Live a God focused life.

Prepare for eternity.

Use your gift from God to serve others.

Live a life driven by God's grace.

Don't Wait to Love.

Love God with all of your heart,
mind and soul.

Love others unselfishly.

Love is eternal.

Love leaves a legacy.

It was only a sunny smile and little
it cost in the giving

But like the morning light it
scattered the night

And made the day worth living.

Anonymous

The precepts of the
LORD are right, giving
joy to the heart. The
commands of the LORD
are radiant, giving light
to the eyes.

Psalm 19:8

Jesus did not come to make God's love possible, but to make God's love visible.

Author Unknown

Maybe what you're waiting for hasn't been listed. It's important to make your life one in which you are giving and not always taking.

Instead, it should be that of your inner self, the unfading beauty of a gentle and quiet spirit, which is of great worth in God's sight.

1 Peter 3:4

Live a life where you are not the central focus but where you make God the center of your life. Look around at everything you take for granted and realize how each of these things are a gift and none should be taken lightly.

As we work long hard hours in order to give our children things we never had, we should also not forget to give our children the things we did have. Don't Wait to give your children all the love and morality to which we were exposed.

Life is like going to school because we continually learn. Our examination doesn't come until the end of our life. It's not here that people ask for their awards and diplomas. We don't desire any worldly object. We want to see people we love. It is at this time that we realize that relationships are what life is all about.

After experiencing the death of my dad, my aunt seven months later, and then the death of my mother, I've learned how fragile life is and that eternal life is the greatest gift God offers us. It's all that will stand the test of time.

I run in the path of your commands, for you have set my heart free.

Psalm 119:32

The soft sweet summer was warm and glowing
Bright were the blossoms on every bough
I trusted him when the roses were blooming
I trust him now.

Anonymous

But as for me and my household, we will serve the LORD.

Joshua 24:15

When we make space for God in our life, we have a whole new beginning. We discover what we need to focus on in our life as we read God's word. Our priorities change as we feel God guiding us in the pattern He planned.

Drop a stone into the water in a moment it is gone.
But there are a hundred ripples circling on and on.
Say a word of cheer and splendor in a moment it is gone.
But there are a hundred ripples circling on and on.

Anonymous

Don't Wait

Discipline and persistence
in the study of God's word
keeps us focused on what is
important.

GOD LOVES YOU!

JESUS DIED FOR YOU!

However, I consider my life worth nothing to me, if only I may
finish the race and complete the task the Lord Jesus has given
me—the task of testifying to the gospel of God's grace.

Acts 20:24

The best use of your life is to love. The greatest gift you can give is your life surrendered to God.

How do you want to finish the race of your life? Don't Wait . . . take the first step now and change your life forever.

One may give without loving, but none can love without giving.

Anonymous

finish the race.

Don't Wait

Be content with your surroundings, but not with yourself until you have made the most of them.

Anonymous

For God so loved the world that He gave his one and only Son, that whoever believes in Him shall not perish but have eternal life.

John 3:16

Accept Jesus!

The best decision you'll ever make is to
accept Jesus as your Lord and Savior. Take
the first step—leave your legacy—
DON'T WAIT ACCEPT JESUS!

The promise is for you and your children and for all who are far off—for all whom the Lord our God will call.

Acts 2:39

Look for the Don't Wait journal in your favorite bookstore. This journal will keep your spiritual journey alive. Through writing lifes lessons, the clarity of how God is working in your life will be revealed. These lessons can be passed on for generations to come

You can also follow Jane's journey in her upcoming books:

Don't Wait Accept Jesus
Photography and Poetry by Jane

Share your "Don't Wait" story by contacting us using the information below.

Online
www.dontwait.com

Traditional Mail
MaryMark Publishing
P.O. Box 907
Carmel, Indiana 46082

A saint is not one who falls; it is one who gets up and goes on everytime he falls.

Anonymous

SPECIAL
MY HEART,
...UE ALWAYS
...E THAN
...MOM, ALWAYS
...F OTHERS
...RSELF.

...AST COUPLE
...HAVE BEEN
...FOR ALL

...T HAD
...ING END.
HIM AT THE
BE

I AM SO GRATEFUL
THAT GOD HAS BEEN
SO GOOD TO YOU AND
YOU HAVE HAD GOOD
HEALTH. I PRAY YOU
WILL ALWAYS BE WELL.
THANKS FOR BEING
WITH ME ON MY
BIRTHDAY AND THANKS
AGAIN FOR ALL YOU'VE
DONE FOR ME AND
MY FAMILY!
I LOVE YOU!
MOM,
JANEY

We encourage you to take your first step by
sending someone our free e-mail card.

Maybe you would like to share Jesus, or tell
someone you're sorry, or maybe you just want
to tell someone how much you love them. Visit
us at www.dontwait.com and choose the card of
choice. If you don't have e-mail, let us know and
we will send you a card to mail.